Agenda 2021-2030 Exposed

Vaccine Chips & Passports, The Great reset & The New Normal; Unreported & Real News

Rebel Press Media

Disclaimer

Our other books

Check out our other books for other unreported news, exposed facts and debunked truths, and more.

Join the exclusive Rebel Press Media Circle!

You will get a new updates about the unreported reality delivered in your inbox every Friday.

Sign up here today:

https://campsite.bio/rebelpressmedia

Introduction

Archbishop says 'Deep State' and 'Deep Church' work hand in hand to establish anti-Christian world empire - Close cooperation Vatican with China 'a shameful betrayal of the Church's mission'

The "Great Reset - Build Back Better" agenda as it is now being rolled out across the West comes to nothing less than the "establishment of the kingdom of Antichrist," according to Archbishop Carlo Maria Viganò. In recent months, Viganò, one of Pope Francis' fiercest opponents, has repeatedly spoken out in strong terms about what is being done under the guise of fighting a virus. For example, he called the colossal election fraud in the U.S. an "attack of darkness on humanity," and in the fall of 2020 he wrote a letter to Donald Trump warning the president that the Great Reset is a "global conspiracy against humanity and against God.

Table of Contents

Disclaimer 1

Our other books.. 2

Introduction... 3

Table of Contents 4

Chapter 1: The new leader 5

Chapter 2: Exposing the truth........................... 9

Chapter 3: The deep church 12

Chapter 4: Rebuilding society 17

Chapter 5: Vaccines exposed 23

Chapter 6: Psychological terror and war against humanity 26

Chapter 7: Agenda 2021 summarized............. 45

Chapter 1: The new leader

Roman Catholic Pope Francis is the "spiritual leader of the new universal globalist religion.

The Archbishop spoke, among other things, about the central role that he believes China plays in the global 'Deep State'. China wants to expand its economic power around the world, and at home meanwhile "restore Maoist tyranny. This requires the abolition of religions (especially the Catholic ones). These will be replaced by the religion of the State, which has much in common with the universal globalist religion, of which Bergoglio (Pope Francis) is the spiritual leader.'

Viganò consistently calls Pope Francis by his real name, since he does not recognize him as the real pope. Benedict was allegedly deposed by the 'Deep Church' and replaced by the Jesuit Bergoglio, receiving direct help from the Obama administration. That conspiracy was demonstrated by WikiLeaks, which published the hacked emails of Hillary Clinton and John Podesta*, her husband Bill's former chief of staff and later briefly an advisor to Obama.

(John Podesta was one of the central figures in the infamous 'pedo-pizza gate', which was dismissed by the media as a conspiracy theory, but which was abundantly clear from the hacked emails).*

Close cooperation between the Vatican and China 'is a grave betrayal of the Church'

'The complicity of Bergoglio's Deep Church in this diabolical project has robbed Chinese Catholics of the imperishable defense that the papacy always was for them. Until Benedict XVI, the papacy has refused to enter into any agreements with the dictatorship in Beijing... Suspicions that China was involved in Benedict's resignation are very strong, and are consistent with the picture as we have seen it develop in recent months.'

'As a result, we now face a shameful betrayal of the mission of the Church of Christ, carried out by its highest leaders, in open conflict with the members of the Chinese Catholic underground hierarchy who have remained faithful to our Lord and His Church.' He hopes, therefore, that there are still governments left in the world that have not been corrupted and undermined by the Deep State, and that they care about the fate of the faithful in China and take action. *(At least in the West, those governments are no longer there)*

The close cooperation between the Vatican and China is "a serious betrayal of the Church by its leaders. We could also assume that in some cases this betrayal is committed not only by individuals, but also by the institutions themselves, as is the case with the European Union, which is currently finalizing a commercial agreement with China, despite the systematic violation of human rights and violent repression of dissenters in that country.' *(And perhaps this is also because the EU has been busy for many years making itself a copy of China in technocratic-authoritarian terms).*

Joe Biden is an 'unimaginable disaster' for the world, 'the man serves an anti-Christian agenda'

Joe Biden in the White House means, according to the archbishop, 'an irreparable disaster' for the world. At the same time, "he is indisputably just a puppet in the hands of the elite, who are ready to remove him as soon as they decide to replace him with Kamala Harris. Biden's far-left vice president, it should be noted, is regularly addressed as "president" by Biden himself. The demented Biden, who can barely utter two full sentences in a row without losing the thread, will therefore be aware himself that he will presumably be replaced by Harris during his first term in office, who will permanently turn the US into a steely communist climate-vaccine dictatorship, just as is now happening in the EU.

'Bergoglio's subservience to the globalist agenda is clear, as is his active support for Joe Biden.' This is why the current pope was so hostile to Trump, 'who in his eyes was an obstacle that needed to be removed so that the Great Reset can be set in motion... Joe Biden serves the globalist ideology and its perverse, anti-human, anti-Christian, diabolical agenda.'

Chapter 2: Exposing the truth

'Corruption and crimes by leaders of the Church must be revealed'

To stop the Deep Church and restore the Catholic Church, "the extent of the involvement of the leaders of the Church with the Masonic globalist project must be revealed, and the nature of the corruption and crimes committed by these men. Under Francis, he says, the Church has been "taken over by mercenaries.

Catholics, however, still have, in his view, 'time to stop this global overthrow, and the establishment of the New Order. Let them think about what kind of future they want for the coming generations, and the destruction of society. Let them think about their responsibility to God, their children, and their nation.

However, he said this at a time when some were still hoping that the illegal electoral coup in the US could still be reversed, and Biden kept out of the White House. If that did not succeed, however, "the U.S. will be wiped out of history.

The mainstream media is an indispensable ally of the Deep State

'The Great Reset plan uses the mainstream media as an indispensable ally; the (Western) media companies are almost all an active part of the Deep State, and know that the power guaranteed to them in the future depends exclusively on their slavish submission to this agenda.'

That the opponents of the Great Reset are invariably called 'conspiracy theorists' is, he says, 'confirmation of the existence of that conspiracy, and of the fact that its implementers are very dismayed that this has been discovered and told to the public. Yet they themselves say that nothing will remain the same ("the new normal"), and "Build Back Better," to make us believe that the radical changes they want to impose are necessary because of pandemic, climate change, and technological advances.

Years ago, the term "New (World) Order" was labeled "conspiracy thinking," but now all world leaders, including the Pope, are speaking openly about it, proposing exactly such a global totalitarian system that so-called "conspiracy thinkers" have been warning about for so long. Figures like Klaus Schwab (WEF) and Bill Gates are not even ashamed to say that a pandemic was needed to push through this 'Great Reset', this total reversal of our society, with the full cooperation of the national governments.

The foundation for a future society without parents, without religion, and the imposition of a devilish cult'

If they succeed in gaining total control over our countries, then we will have a society with 'families without father and mother, polyamory, sodomy, children who can change their sex, the abolition of religion and the imposition of a devilish cult, abortion and euthanasia, the abolition of private property, a 'health' (vaccine) dictatorship, and an eternal pandemic. Is this the world we want, that you want for yourself, your children, your family and friends?'

'We must all become aware of how much the proponents of this New World Order and the Great Reset hate the inalienable values of our Greek-Christian civilization, such as religion, the family, respect for life and the inviolable rights of the human individual, and national sovereignty.'

Chapter 3: The deep church

'A group of conspirators was and still is active in the heart of the Church for the interests of the elite. Most of them are visible, but the most dangerous are those who do not show themselves, who are never mentioned in the newspapers. They will not hesitate to force Bergoglio to resign if he does not follow their orders, just as they did with Ratzinger. They want to turn the Vatican into a retirement home for emeritus popes, destroy the papacy, and seize power - exactly the same thing that is happening in the Deep State, where Biden is the equivalent of Bergoglio.'

'To overthrow the Deep State and Deep Church, three things are necessary:

We must become aware of the globalist plan, and the extent to which it is instrumental to the establishment of the kingdom of Antichrist, since it shares the same principles, means and objectives;

Second, we must firmly reject this diabolical plan, and ask the pastors of the Church - as well as ordinary believers - to defend it and break their complicit silence: God will otherwise demand accountability from them for their apostasy;

Finally, it is necessary to pray and ask the Lord to give each of us strength to resist the ideological tyranny that is daily imposed on us, not only by the media, but also by the cardinals and bishops who are under Bergoglio's thumb.'

If we prove that we stand firm in this temptation, if we... do not allow ourselves to be seduced by "false Christs and false prophets," then the Lord will give us - at least for the moment - the defeat of the attack of the children of darkness on God and men. But if, out of fear, we follow the prince of this world ... we will be condemned along with him to inexorable defeat and eternal damnation.'

'I shudder for those who do not realize this responsibility to God for the souls entrusted to them. But to those who fight courageously to defend the rights of God, the nation and family (of believers), the Lord assures His protection.'

Do you sometimes believe that Satan's followers are honest and sincere?

'You have not failed in this battle, since it is your sacred duty to make your own contribution by taking the side of Good. Others, addicted to corruptions, or blinded by an infernal hatred of our Lord, have chosen the side of Evil.'

'Do not think that the children of darkness operate in an honest manner, nor be shocked that they make use of deception. Or do you sometimes believe that Satan's followers are honest, sincere and loyal? The Lord has warned us about the devil, who "was a murderer of men from the beginning, and stands not in truth, for there is no truth in him. When he speaks the lie, he speaks according to his nature, for he is a liar and the father of lies.' (John 8:44)

Pick up your spiritual weapons now that hell seems to be winning

'Now that the gates of hell seem to be winning, allow me to appeal to you. I trust you to respond to it immediately and generously. I ask you to put your trust in God, an act of humility and brotherly devotion to the Lord of Hosts.... Pray with an honest soul, with a pure heart, with the assurance that you will be heard and heard. Pray that the forces of Evil will be defeated, and the powers of Good will prevail.'*

Vigano calls on all believers of all ages to pray and to take up their "spiritual weapons, which Satan and his minions will have to retreat from furiously... Do not be discouraged by the deceptions of the Enemy, especially in this terrible time when blatant lies and frauds are taunting Heaven. If you pray in faith, the days of our adversaries will be numbered.'

Does a "spiritual rebirth" stand a chance?

In conclusion, the Archbishop hopes that people worldwide will speak with one voice in their churches, homes and streets, and unite spiritually to fight and win this spiritual battle so that there will be 'a spiritual rebirth' not only in the U.S., but all over the world.

However, this will require something that has never been achieved up to now, namely that people look beyond their own religious or ideological frameworks, respect each other's different and divergent views and opinions, and focus together on the common goal of not allowing this world to fall definitively into the hands of the globalist forces of Evil, which have begun their final seizure of power since this year, and are now imposing their climate-virus dictatorship on humanity at an unrelenting pace.

So far, we can see that the old "divide and conquer" tactic is unfortunately working perfectly even among the awake and waking part of the population. The moment we start imposing on each other that we must necessarily look at something or explain it in this or that way, that we must use these or those terms, and that we are otherwise 'wrong', we have no chance. And then you can hope and pray until you are blue in the face, but that will have absolutely no effect, since every real change starts with yourself.

Chapter 4: Rebuilding society

Millions of Christians and conservatives who voted for Trump need to be forcibly 're-educated' - America hasn't been a Christian country for a long time, and the churches have themselves to thank for that too.

An influential group of Democratic delegates is backing a document from the Secular Democrats of America demanding that he silence the "white and Christian right," erase the country's "biblical principles," and renounce the "Judeo-Christian basis" of society. In a speech, President Obama once declared that "America is no longer a Christian nation. Biden seems to be definitively taking care of that. What will take its place is a Marxist, UN-subordinate climate-vaccine dictatorship - just like in Europe.

That Biden himself has much in common with the far-left anti-Christian agenda is beyond dispute. On September 15, 2018, he literally called a portion of the Christian right that had voted for Trump two years earlier "the dregs of society.

Among the call supported by at least 13 Democratic delegates is Rashida Tlaib, who covered herself in a Palestinian flag in the last election, vowing that 'we are going to depose this M..F.. (Trump) is going to depose". Another promoter, Steve Cohen, has ties to the Memphis Socialist Party USA, and to members of

Liberation Road, a pro-Chinese communist organization. Co-founder Jamie Raskin wrote articles for the Democratic Socialists of America.

Traditional Christians would have 'sectarian, dangerous' influence

According to Brannon Howse, a conservative radio host, the Democrats have a problem not with churches in general, but with 'right-wing' churches, which hold to traditional Biblical principles. 'As long as you preach the left-wing progressive socialist religion they think it's fine, but if you preach something based on Judeo-Christian values, they want to take you down.'

The drafters even demand that Biden openly break with the term "Judeo-Christian," and act against the "sectarian, dangerous influence" of Christians in government. Conservative America's opposition to abortion, stem cell research and the carbon/climate agenda is called part of a "cultural war" against "science. Trump and the Christian community are also blamed for the allegedly 'hundreds of thousands of deaths' caused by Covid-19.

Christians stand in the way of communist America

Author and filmmaker Trevor Loudon, who has been involved with the left for decades, pointed out that

Christians are demonized in the document as "nationalists" with an "extremist, sectarian" and "white supremacist" agenda. 'This can be taken as a recommendation to send conservative Christians to re-education camps,' Loudon said. 'They talk about re-educating and reprogramming traditional Christians, who from their point of view are dangerous people, racists and nationalists.'

'What they're really saying is that they want to brainwash you with their ideas. The communists would be proud of this document... The Democratic party is now a Marxist party. This document is directed against the greatest enemy of the Marxists in this country, and that is traditional Christianity. That's very clear.'

'Leftists and communists already control Hollywood (the film and entertainment industry), education, the media, and most institutions. The only thing they don't control are conservative Bible-believing Christians, who voted for Reagan at the time, and now for Trump.'

Christians prevented the elite's dream candidate, Hillary Clinton, from becoming president. 'She should have completed the communistization of America... So, the left understands that they have to suppress Christianity, or pervert it in their own direction.'

In the writings, these "Secular Democrats of America" call on Biden to:

* Cut off all funding for pregnancy crisis centers and educational programs that promote sexual abstinence;

* End freedom of religious expression, repeal the Religious Freedom Restoration Act (RFRA), and rescind the federal religious freedom protections put in place by Trump;

* Make vaccinations mandatory for children, and take away parents' say in the matter;

* Remove the term "In God We Trust" from physical U.S. dollars;

* Ending Trump's support for adoption and foster agencies that operate on religious principles;

* Provide high subsidies for 'comprehensive sex education' to school children, including promoting many dozens of types of 'genders';

* Oppose 'Project Blitz,' which promotes traditional family values and would undermine the LGBTQ agenda;

* To stop using the term "Judeo-Christian values" because tens of millions of Americans would no longer feel represented by it.

Under the Biden-Harris regime, as in China, churches will likely only be allowed to continue to exist if they preach the "party line" unabridged and uncritical, or in other words, hold their followers to absolute obedience to the government and government policies. This means that there will no longer be a place for churches and believers who continue to adhere to classic Christian values concerning God, love of country, family and the inviolability of the individual.

America has not been a Christian country for a very long time

Finally, we would like to note that the U.S. has actually not been a Christian country (anymore) for a long time. Numerous presidents who identified themselves as 'Christian' have waged bloody wars, the penultimate of which, Barack Obama, even caused 10 x more civilian casualties than his reviled predecessor George Bush. The hatred that Muslim extremists harbor towards Christians and Christianity is largely caused by this, and thus quite understandable.

A president who sits in church on Sunday, and on Monday gives the order to bomb your country and plunge it into chaos, and who does not consider a few civilian casualties more or less, is certainly not an advertisement for the Christian faith. The same can be said about the enormous wealth and greed that characterizes American politicians, bankers and businessmen.

In addition, a large part of "normal" Christian America has also come to focus on the pursuit of money, wealth, success, prosperity and health (the false "gospel of happiness," as Corry ten Boom called it). This self-centered, essentially raped gospel, preached by many 'mega churches', was spread around the world after World War II, and has poisoned not only virtually all Western churches (to a greater or lesser extent), but also those in South America, Africa and large parts of Asia.

Thus, predominantly hypocritical American Christianity has completely eroded itself, as it were, and will have to reap the bitter fruits of this under the Biden-Harris regime. This is not a pleasant prospect, but it will separate the wheat from the chaff among Christians, especially if it turns out that the escapist theology of prosperity, which was maintained for years that believers do not have to go through (the) tribulation here, was a blatant lie.

Transhuman man to be integrated with global digital control system, 'Implantable 5G nanotech biosensor as early as 2021 in Covid-19 vaccines'

The Pentagon's technology development arm, DARPA, and the Bill & Melinda Gates Foundation are collaborating with the tech company Profusa in the development of an implantable nanotech biosensor made of hydrogel (substance similar to a soft contact lens). This biosensor, which is smaller than a grain of rice, can be injected along with a vaccine and is applied just under the skin, where it actually merges with your body. The nanotech component allows for remote monitoring of all information about yourself, your body and your health via 5G. The biosensor, which can also receive information and commands, is expected to be approved by the FDA in early 2021 - just in time for the planned global Covid-19 vaccination campaign.

DefenseOne wrote about this hydrogel biosensor back in March, which is "inserted under the skin with a hypodermic needle. Among other things, it contains a specially designed molecule that sends out a fluorescent signal once the body starts fighting an infection. The electronic part attached to (/in) the skin detects this signal, and then sends an alert to a doctor, a website, or a government agency. 'It's like a blood lab on the skin that can pick up, even before there are other symptoms like coughing, the body's response to illness.'

It is therefore not difficult to guess why this sensor may be considered of great importance by the elite in the (so-called) fight against Covid-19. Anyone who has this - irremovable - biosensor injected into their body will be quarantined by the government at the slightest infection, and may be subject to other coercive measures, even if the person in question is not sick at all, nor shows any symptoms of it.

Biosensor monitors all body functions and transmits them via 5G

By using hydrogel, the biosensor will not be seen by the body as an intruder and attacked, but rather integrate with it. Also, according to the company, the sensor can not only detect infections, but also monitor the oxygen and glucose levels in your blood, as well as your hormone levels, your heart rate, your breathing, your body temperature, your sex life, your emotions - in short, EVERYTHING. Through 5G, all this information can soon be transmitted to every medical and political authority.

Profusa is currently conducting a study with Imperial College, also funded by Bill Gates, which became infamous for its ridiculous predictions of doom regarding Covid-19, which soon turned out to be utterly bogus. However, it was based on these that the lockdowns, social distancing, and the associated partial destruction of the economy and the elimination of many civil liberties were made.

Transhuman humans to be integrated with global digital control system

The biosensor, which may therefore be incorporated into Covid-19 vaccines as early as 2021, comes very close to realizing the aspiration of a transhuman human, in which everyone is totally controllable and even steerable. The "new human," or the human 2.0 as envisioned by the tech elite around Bill Gates and Elon Musk, will be gradually transformed into a kind of cyborg between now and 2025-2030, and become an integral - and therefore irreversible - part of a global digital control system, in which personal freedoms will have completely disappeared, and even human free will, will have been taken away.

Not for nothing do we call this the system of "the Beast. For the first time in history, technology has advanced to the point where the biblical prophecies about the 'sign of the Beast' can be fully carried out and fulfilled.

Chapter 6: Psychological terror and war against humanity

'Before 2020, our rulers, the 1% percent, only demanded your physical labor; now they want to invade and take full control over your body' - 'There is still hope for us if you stop participating and build new communities'

Democracy has been abolished, the rule of law no longer functions. There is talk of a real 'war against the people', carried out by our own governments, which in turn are controlled by the big tech companies. This is the start of 'techno-fascism' and a 'transhumanist dictatorship', which is being imposed on the people with the help of psychological terror measures (lockdowns, mouthguards, curfews, vaccinations).

Daily propaganda to keep people obedient

Pointing out that the measures were originally only supposed to last a few months, but now, over a year later, are still being enforced and are being further expanded despite increasing protests from scientists, doctors, economists and other experts. The governments, however, do not listen at all to these dissenting voices, and going to court no longer makes sense anywhere, as judges are only there to give government policies a legal stamp.

In Germany, resistance to the measures seems to be better and more organized. That resistance is not futile and clearly has an effect. We can see that "from the enormous propaganda they have to deliver every day. Without that propaganda they would never be able to get away with this madness.' Whether that resistance will eventually mean the end of the governments, however, remains to be seen.

Citizens' rights sidelined with 'unbridled insolence'

The center of the problem is that the separation of powers has disappeared, and with it the basis of democracy. This has not been functioning for much longer. That process began especially after the neoliberal counterrevolution some 30 years ago. This has created a power cartel of parties that actually only pursue the same goals.

What is special about these times is the "uninhibited insolence with which our governments are now setting aside the law. The constant state of exception in the West is 'classic proof that the rule of law has been destroyed.' Top Nazi jurist and propagandist Karl Schmidt had already defined this state of exception in his book Politische Theologie. Whoever controls the state of exception also controls the people. He pointed out that this situation could also be staged.

Permanent state of exception; 'you have nothing more to say'

Schmidt made a distinction from a state of emergency, such as a flood. A state of emergency is always temporary, but a state of exception can last much longer. In fact, our governments are now making this state of exception that has been in place since 2020 permanent. 'They have staged this state of affairs with corona. In short, you can say that democracy has been suspended, has been abolished.'

'They know that those mouthguards are total nonsense, numerous studies confirm it. But you have nothing more to say. You have to shut up, that's essentially the constitution-breaking message. With that comes all kinds of physical oppression. The psychological oppression is much worse.'

The rejection of corona measures in the former East Germany is, thanks to the communist past, 'much more deeply embedded in the population than in the completely degenerated West,' although there are all kinds of initiatives there too (such as Querdenken). The mass media play a very bad role in the current oppressive corona dictatorship, also by promoting the Cold War 2.0 (against Russia). 'They are now playing the same disgraceful, disgusting role with corona as heels of the government apparatus, the multinationals and the financial industry.'

Virus instrument for triggering Great Reset

'People have chosen the virus as an instrument for a new reign, what is called the 'Fourth Industrial Revolution', the Great Reset.' The aforementioned neoliberal revolution was the beginning of this. It put an end to social capitalism, in which the citizens were still allowed to benefit from the growing wealth and prosperity. That's why, on the whole, people in the West were a lot happier in the 1970s than they are now.

Thanks to the (neo)liberals the state stopped working primarily for the citizens and started working primarily for the multinationals and financial industry. In those 30 years exactly what neocon Zbigniew Brzezinski (with admittedly different wording) had planned was done, namely the deliberate dumbing down of the broad population ('dumbing down') with mindless entertainment on TV and the like. Meanwhile, our governments were taken over. Without the population noticing, their governments internally 'redefined' themselves.

Market radicalism: Causers of the crisis were rewarded, the people had to bleed

From 2007-2008 (Lehman Brothers collapse, financial crisis) market radicalism broke out in full force. Those who caused the crisis, the banks and speculators, the organized criminals who had committed gigantic (financial) crimes and had squandered trillions, simply told the governments that they were 'too big to fail', and that the people should therefore pay for the mess they had caused. Then they just went on with their practices, up to the present day. Our governments made this possible, and are still making this possible.

This expropriation of the people's and state's wealth also took place through privatizations. The power of the multinational corporations grew more and more, precisely because they were deregulated. They were no longer restricted, they could do whatever they wanted. As tax revenues fell and the debts of states rose, these corporations were then able to take over almost everything (health care, public transport, roads, etc.).

'Step-by-step coup'

'An incremental coup d'etat is a very good description for this.' But still it wasn't enough for those in power today. Now they are saying that globalization - including spotty air travel and moving production to East Asia, which necessitated huge transport flows - cannot go on like this. The same people who caused this are now carrying out the Great Reset, and once again the painful consequences of this are only being passed on to the ordinary population.

One of the big drivers, Klaus Schwab (World Economic Forum), literally called corona a "window of opportunity" (and acknowledged that this virus is no more dangerous than the flu). Nevertheless, he vowed that society may never return to normal).

Collective degeneration? Up to 90% of people have allowed themselves to be frightened

It is "mind-boggling how easily the public is played with" and accepts it all. Two weapons are being used against the people; fear, and the media. 'You can't say otherwise than that they have executed this fear game perfectly. What we don't understand is how it is possible to drive 85% to 90% of the population into this state of fear.' Ensign suggests as a possible cause that there may have been 'collective degeneration well before the corona crisis.'

Recent studies confirm that neoliberalism has caused a huge 'mental damage' in people's minds, a form of welfare blunting. If you enjoy too much prosperity, you become lazy and weak. There is no longer a need to make an effort and to keep thinking about other ideas and options, to stay alert. You are taken care of by the state anyway, is the feeling. Or you have a fine job, even though workers are under increasing pressure and stress.

The fear pyschology was fueled with increasing so-called catastrophes (climate, energy, nature, etc.). Also, well over 100 military (NATO) exercises take place every year because Russia and China would like to cause World War III. Therefore, society was already quite steeped in permanent fear, only to be dealt the final blow with corona.

People in positions have always been followers.

Not only the general public, but also doctors, physicians and scientists, who know very well that corona is not a major threat at all, have nevertheless supported this policy. "The mass of people in positions have always been followers. Don't be under any illusions; we had a high position in the civil service for 10 years... Well, before you get in you have to renounce your intellect. The idiots at the top just say that 'if we say that white wall is red, then it is red'.

In short, almost all of these experts are now choosing the safest path. If you want to survive, keep your job and position, you have to go along with everything. With that comes a lot of opportunism and self-submission, 'and in fact self-denial.' In health care, very many employees do see what is really going on.'

Government leaders invariably invoke 'science,' but 'I don't think there is that much corruption anywhere else.' We then point out that there are also many scientists who do make well-founded objections, but they are simply ignored. More than 250 of the best scientists, including the world's top virologist John Ioannidis, are simply not listened to. Or worse: they are persecuted.

Democracy abolished, government has become lawless and disenfranchised

The behaviour of the police in the West literally reminds us of 'Gestapo times'. 'Again; democracy has been abolished, and those in government are permitting themselves every brutality you can imagine. Take, for example, the curfew. The judge rejects it, and four hours later the government commits a new dirty trick. What is this!" Ensign: "So that means there's actually lawlessness?

"Yes, absolutely! Lawlessness, lawlessness, violation of the constitution, it's nothing else anymore.' Ensign: 'The laws only go one way anymore: to dictate to the people, and conversely they no longer offer any legal protection.' All the boundaries of an intact justice have fallen away.

Ensign then cites the article in Common Sense titled "The German Tyrant," in which the sociologist writes that "they are the enemies of humanity. Merkel hates Germany and the German people. That certainly has to do with her growing up in the (GDR) dictatorship. She was the ideal candidate for a creeping government putsch in Germany. Such figures are not deployed without the approval of the Transatlantic actors or the US.' Ensign says this is true of all Western countries, and our governments are 'effectively collaborators with the enemy'.

'9/11 was the beginning of the war against its own people'

The governments collaborate against their own peoples... we have come to the point of saying that they wage war against the peoples... This form of warfare began with 9/11. It was directed first outward, to destroy the Middle East. But it also gave a perverse message to its own people. The Department of Homeland Security became a kind of second Pentagon, but for one's own country, with all the civil rights and fundamental rights abrogations, taking away the freedom of citizens, as a result.'

Then the number of terror attacks in Europe exploded, which was a further form of fearmongering ('Operation Gladio' in Europe, a deliberate intelligence-driven and executed 'strategy of tension').

However, terror attacks were not yet having sufficient effect, so they wanted something with which to keep the population in systematic fear. That became corona, 'the crown (corona) of the Western elite', 'the complete imprisonment of the peoples by this corona (pandemic*) hoax'... As organized criminals you can't do better.' 'You could admire it if it wasn't so evil.'

Now to carry this out to perfection required years of preparation (for example, with Event 201 in October 2019). That also included swine flu (swine flu) and bird flu. Ensign: 'So we are up against a very well-organized enemy of humanity?' 'Yes, absolutely.' Ensign: 'So do we still have a chance?'

They want to plunge us and future generations into absolute debt bondage

'That's the big, exciting question,'. We can't expect anything more from our governments. They have certainly had no choice since Corona. They are working on the 'total indebtedness' of all states, using corona as an excuse. Deutsche Bank already got the green light from Merkel for 1.9 trillion euros in loans in April 2020. 'Their main goal: to plunge the next generations into absolute debt slavery, and to own all the still vital parts ('assets', think in NL of SMEs and farmers).'

Corrupt politicians have personally profited enormously from all these neoliberal privatizations. They only wanted to make a career and did not look at any other interest. 'Look at politics, there are so many zeros in there now. Don't kid yourself about that. And what does a zero have to lose? They have everything to gain. Who wants to participate in a political party now?

There is hardly any political ideology left, only the perpetuation of positions of power,' says Stuurman. Hence the infamous revolving door effect: people from politics often end up in big business and banks (and sometimes vice versa). It is all about us and us alone. Qualifications and achievements are no longer important.

International conglomerates and NGOs have taken over the government "like a cancer

International bodies and NGOs (*especially in the fields of globalization and climate*) have then 'like a cancerous tumor' penetrated the government, and have had it draft and implement laws against its own people, its own country and its own companies. Meanwhile, this government apparatus gobbles up billions. This would still be justifiable if they actually wanted to do something for the people, but that is no longer the case.

Then there is the example of the 600 billion that has been spent on corona measures in Europe alone. Meanwhile, it is still claimed that there is too little hospital capacity. 'But for that 130 billion, we could have rebuilt the entire healthcare system five times over, including staff. But not a cent was spent on that!' It's an incomparable process of destruction. They are engaged in destruction from morning to night.'

People who can't and don't want to live like this anymore in our anti-democratic states have to start looking after their own interests. They have to start uniting, keep protesting and demonstrating, separate themselves as much as possible from current politics, and stop watching and following all the mainstream media, because they only condemn any dissent.

10% - 20% of humanity will create a new path

The population may be falling apart into two groups, 'but that division has been there for a long time,' You used to be able to talk to people about many things, but since Corona that has stopped. A schism has taken place that runs straight through friends, colleagues and families. They don't understand anything anyway. You can tell them what you want, point to the expertise of other scientists, but they just don't want to hear it. Every other sound is called 'nonsense', while they themselves have not even investigated it.

'They don't read anything! There have been excellent publications (by reputable scientists) in recent months, but they don't care.' From that part of the population, we can expect nothing more. 'We are left with 10% -

20%. If they all become active, the government has a real problem. All remaining possibilities must be exhausted to stop this criminal policy.

Furthermore, those 20% must develop a new way of life, and accept that this entails much more risk. The biggest problem is that we do not have our own closed territory (*a kind of 'free state'*), so whether you live in Germany, the Netherlands, France, Italy or England, you will be persecuted. Ensign: 'Is there any room for any optimism then?'

'Everything that makes life fun these supercriminals have destroyed'

'In the big picture, I don't see that. I don't think we can turn this around within one or two years.' Everyone should therefore become and remain active in their own field - doctors, scientists, publicists, journalists, etc. - become and remain active, and connect with each other. Mies reiterates his enormous surprise at the cooperation of SMEs (hospitality, entertainment, events, sports, tourism, shopkeepers, etc.) with their own destruction. 'Everything that makes life fun these super criminals have destroyed.'

Tens of thousands of businesses bankrupt, hundreds of thousands of people unemployed, and still no resistance? Yet it only takes 2 or 3 million determined people to go to Berlin, and 'Merkel can pack it in then. She'll have a hard time getting away. We're also baffled that so many companies are locking themselves in, just because the minister says so. 'Do you know why they are participating? Because they are structurally conservative. Most SME'ers and also freelancers have never been rebellious people.' Automatic obedience to the government is in their system. To date, this prevents them from rebelling en masse.

Qualitative contacts instead of social rattling

Despite the bad situation, there is something very positive, namely that we have gotten to know like-minded people and have been able to establish contact with them on a completely different, high quality level. They no longer talk about nonsense like they did with old and out-of-touch contacts (the 'social chatter', i.e., the soccer results, yesterday's TV programs, news about BN people, the new lease car, etc.). That is pure profit.

But major concerns do exist, such as about the upcoming corona and vaccination passports, which will exclude people who have not been tested and/or vaccinated. Still, 'the more pressure that will be put on the population, the greater the resistance will be. That's already the case.'

'People who taunt conspiracy theorists don't read anything themselves anymore'

We can only recommend Klaus Schwab's latest book about Covid-19 to people who say that. All dystopian developments are in it, including population control and reduction, new technologies, ID2020, everything is connected, from early to late you are under total control. If people then still claim that we are the conspiracy theorists, we can only say that in the minds of those people nothing functions at all.'

Stuurman also sees that the people who talk about conspiracy theories have not read up and do not know what it is about. But they can read it themselves from the executors of this real conspiracy, like Klaus Schwab! They shouldn't be so lazy! That's all.'

Techno-fascism: the end of humanity as we know it

What Schwab wants, the Great Reset 'is a kind of techno-fascism, a tyranny, a trans-humanist dictatorship. They want to enter your body. That's the new profit regime, the new capitalism. They used to use your labor power, now they want to get IN you. They want to implant and inject something into you... They are connecting everything together. First comes 5G, then 6G, and then just see what happens next. In the background, this is military technology.'

This actually means the end of humanity as a species as it is. As a self-contained species as we knew it, yes... We can speak of the end of humanity as we knew it. They want a hybrid being, a techno-monster, a cyborg, and they think that's great. They then call that an improvement. Yes, for the police, security services and the military it is, but not for humanity.' What they want is a kind of all-encompassing technocratic 'dashboard' with which everyone, down to the last man, woman and child, can be monitored and controlled. That's their plan, that's exactly their idea.

To see what is happening now, we advise everyone to google Albert Biedermann and his 'chart of coercion', which shows exactly how the current rulers work to get us under total control, and also how to keep prisoners of war in check. 'And that's exactly like now: manipulative psychology to the absolute extreme.'

'This is terror, we are being treated like prisoners of war'

'Isolation, monopolization of perception (silencing / ridiculing all critical voices), terrorizing and psychologically exhausting people with a mouth guard requirement, social distancing, the curfew and vaccinations - this is all done on purpose, and of course high penalties and rock-hard action against those who don't comply and/or protest. No mouthguard on? Penalty! Out at night after ten? Punishment! So: TERROR.'

'People are being deprived of using logic,' adds Stuurman. People are no longer allowed to think and judge for themselves. Nothing is judged anymore; they are told what to do and what not to do. And when they sit down in their cage like a frightened rabbit, they are just held up a carrot. And then the frightened bunny says: oh, it's not so bad, is it? They really have our best interests at heart, don't they?

This is nothing but the 'domestication' of the population. 'We are treated as prisoners of war, no longer as human beings. You have to submit. This is open captivity.' At the same time, the victims are made dependent on the perpetrators (Stockholm Syndrome), and at night in front of the TV they hang on to the lips of those who do all this to them.

Don't get more involved in modern society; build new communities

There IS hope, but only 'if you stop participating. Ignore the orders as much as possible,' but you don't have to become a martyr, for example that they invade your home. 'And very important: make new friendships, and if we have to meet in the woods or in a basement, so be it. '

'Try to establish new communities and new villages. Get out of the big cities, they are broken anyway. And as far as possible go back to analog technologies.' So, internet only when needed, and always the latest smartphones and apps is absolutely unnecessary (especially not the corona app). 'So, get maximum independence from the system.'

Chapter 7: Agenda 2021 summarized

'The nation state, freedom and your voice are being completely destroyed' - 'Only mass resistance can stop this anti-human agenda, which is already being implemented'

Café Weltschmerz has published an interview with a recognized top American expert regarding Agenda 21, which can be summarized as a power grab that will eventually place the entire world under one technocratic communist dictatorship, in which individuals and peoples will have no say at all, not even over their own health and lives. With the Covid-19 fear pandemic hoax, the next phase of this de facto coup against our freedom, democracy and right to self-determination has begun. Café Weltschmerz therefore doesn't put "The hidden agenda behind the destruction of our society" under it for nothing - a destruction that is also being deliberately carried out by world governments.

Independent journalist Spiro Kouras (Activist Post) interviewed the executive director of the Post Sustainability Institute, Rosa Koire, an expert on land use and property rights who has given speeches around the world. Her work can be found on the website Democrats United Against UN Agenda21, a website that was inaccessible at the time of writing.

Koire is also the author of the book "Behind the Green Mask - UN Agenda 21. Agenda 21 was signed by 178 countries and the Vatican in 1992. With this agenda, a globalist power elite wants to gain total control over all land, water, vegetation, minerals, construction, means of production, food and energy. Law enforcement, education, information, and the people themselves must also come under this complete control.

Agenda 2030: intermediate step in destruction of nation-state and freedom

Also, large sums of "money" must be moved from the developed to the less developed countries. Ultimately, it's about destroying your ability to have a voice, a representative government.' National governments turn into administrations. 'Your ability to be free and independent is being completely destroyed. The goal is to transfer power from local and individual persons to a global system of government... It is a plan to disrupt and destroy the existing system. It is a plan of transformation and control, and that is what we are experiencing now.'

Agenda 2030 is only an intermediate step in Agenda 21, just as 2020, 2025 and 2050 are. By 2050, with the help and support of big globalist names like Ford, Rockefeller, Soros, Gates, Zuckerberg, Musk, the Pope, and last but not least Rothschild, this perfidious plan must be completed. By 2050, all nation-states are to be abolished, and the world's population concentrated in a number of mega-cities that can encompass entire states and countries (just as the Netherlands, along with Belgium and the German Ruhr, is to become one big city).

'This is meant to crush your ability to control what happens to you. It is a global plan, but it is being implemented locally under different names.' This is done deliberately to divert people's attention from the real objectives.

Actually, everything called 'green' and 'sustainable development' falls under Agenda 21. This includes 'climate change', i.e., all climate accords and initiatives, and certainly Covid-19 . 'A global crisis requires a global response,' is their idea. 'And that warrants global governance.'

Climate change and the corona p(l)andemic 'are designed to send people into a panic, so bad that you literally fear you won't survive it.' Whether or not there really is such a thing as a climate crisis is not even relevant, according to Koire. It works so well, it would have been invented anyway (indeed, it IS invented, conceived, in the early 1990s, which is literally written in UN documents).

The 'Great (Green) Reset'

Skouras then points to the 'Great (Green) Reset' launched at the World Economic Forum in Davos. Koire responds that she 'does not want to be an alarmist' but is very concerned that this 'reset' is now being pushed through regardless of the cost to people and society. 'However, they are staying behind their Green Mask, because once that comes off, the soldier boots and trenches come out.' Literally. See also our December 4, 2019 article: 'UN can use military force against countries that refuse climate agenda' (/ 'UN can shove extreme measures down peoples' throats' - Madrid climate conference participants want tough deals on breaking down prosperity and freedom in Europe).

We have now reached the point where those in power hardly care about the objections and concerns of the people. 'That's a kind of message from them to us, that they no longer really care about us.' It seems that there is not much we can do about it anymore, but Koire believes that it is still possible.

Technology has now advanced to the point where two big goals, eternal life and being able to create life yourself, have come very close. 'These people have no ethical boundary, and that is very worrying. You saw this with the Nazis, with Stalin, and now. There is literally nothing to stop these people.'

Everything and everyone will be digitally connected

In the 'Fourth Industrial Revolution' that they have now set in motion, truly everything and everyone is to be digitally connected. 'They are talking about a new social contract. Well, with a contract, normally both parties have something to say about it. But this is a contract where none of us gets a say... This is one of the reasons why we see all this hysteria in the streets. This is because it's a lesson, a communication to us: this is what happens to you if you take to the streets and dare to stand up against our plan.'

'People ask me: who is doing this to us? That's your government. Your government has been taken over.' With the help of groups and movements such as Antifa and Black Lives Matter, an attempt is being made to spark an uprising. 'We are under attack.' This was the reason Koire turned his back on the Democratic Party. 'But parties are just a distraction. At the top, power knows no party. In this globalist takeover of power, all possible means are being used. The plan is to disrupt and disrupt, and that is what everyone is seeing now. This is the plan to destroy social cohesion, and that is very successful.'

She calls the situation now 'extremely dangerous' because this plan is supported by universities, foundations, companies and government agencies. 'All these parties have been indoctrinated, from kindergarten to university education. These are the 'agents of change' that have been activated.'

'Transformation' = demolition of the individual

The widely used magic word is 'transformation', of education, the economy, the police and society alike. 'Transformation is in reality about breaking down the individual, of your alliance to any 'old' system, such as your family, your 'old' thoughts, or your faith... It is a psychological technique that actually breaks down your personality, and then rebuilds it (according to their new standards).'

The term "institutional racism" also used by the European Government is "just an excuse to literally destroy your mind. Mao Zedong used it, Sung used it, and so did the Nazis. It is a technique by which your personality is broken down, in order to rebuild you as the new human being, the new world citizen.'

Human must merge with A.I.

In this process, A.I. (artificial intelligences) also comes into play. A (global) A.I. police force is coming, not made up of humans. Also, drones will at some point no longer be controlled by humans, but by A.I. 'I don't have to explain that then you get a really dangerous situation.' New Zealand recently officially launched its first A.I. police officer, and in Singapore they are now using intelligent robots to enforce social distancing.

Skouras: 'This is essentially an anti-humanitarian agenda, where they want to merge human with machine (AI).'

By the Covid-19 measures, everyone has been declared a potential enemy of each other. The idea is that you no longer trust even your closest family members and friends. At the same time, our health is also being degraded, which Koire says is a very important part of the Agenda 21 plan. 'This is the plan to inventory and control everything, including your DNA (hence the government's insistence that as many people as possible get tested for Covid-19 - this will allow your DNA to be taken and stored immediately).'

With your 'social credit status' as in China and soon in the US and Europe, you have to 'prove' that you are a loyal and obedient citizen who is 'worthy' of continuing to live in the new order. The system, of course, has been doing this for some time now by favoring certain talented people, which the rest then have to pay for. The Chinese system is going to be rolled out across the planet.

Depopulation vaccine

'The Chinese also agreed in the 1990s to work with the US on a depopulation vaccine.' Did they go through with that? Is that vaccine now out there, and is it being 'sold' to humanity under a different name (perhaps a Covid-19 vaccine?)? Either way, 'depopulation is an essential part of the plan.' If it is determined that you don't have enough value, and/or are taking up too much space, using too much energy, too much water, too much land, then you must be 'isolated' and relocated.

The vast majority of humanity will be forced to live in ('multicultural') mega-cities, where every aspect of our lives will be controlled and managed 24/7/365. 'This plan will literally take all freedom away from you completely. And this is not about a plan for the future, but is something that is already happening right now. So, this is not just in 2030 or 2050. 2020 is really a very important year. A lot of these plans are now being rolled out at the regional level.'

'We have been massively misled by our leaders and their advisors,' said Dr. Mike Yeadon, former vice president at Pfizer, in an interview with Germany's Stiftung Corona Ausschuss just under two weeks ago. 'What I'm about to tell will shock everyone.' Yeadon warned that the constant 'topping up' of corona vaccines, as now seems to be the intention (the 'vaccine subscription' as we once called it last year) is not only totally unnecessary, but also life-threatening, because all these vaccines will not go through the normal approval process. 'Genetic sequences will be injected directly into the arms of hundreds of millions of people... This could cause serious injury and death in a significant proportion of the world's population.'

Immunologist and respiratory organs expert Yeadon - who, by the way, has been away from Pfizer for about 10 years - said he found the 'very large number of deaths' after the corona vaccinations 'no coincidence'. He called it "arrogant" of the vaccine manufacturers to assume that these new vaccines, which instruct the body to produce a spike protein of the corona virus, would not cause major problems, because scientific studies had already shown the danger that this technology would cause a much too strong (auto-)immune response in very many people, which could make them seriously ill or even kill them. The past three months have shown that this is indeed the case.

'All these genetic vaccines (Pfizer-AstraZeneca-Moderna) represent a fundamental safety risk to the population,' he warned.

Because of the poor connection, Dr. Reiner Füllmich, one of the heads of the German committee, summarized what he had said. 'According to Dr. Yeadon, what is happening now is a very serious crime, committed by 'bad actors', our own political and self-proclaimed 'scientific' elite... The spike protein is biologically active, and is precisely replicated by the vaccines. This causes an autoimmune reaction, like a cytokine storm. Several thousand people have already died from this in Europe. In Israel, even 40 times as many people over 80 and 260 times as many younger people have already died from the vaccine than from Covid-19. From all other countries we get similar reports.'

'All vaccines stimulate your body to make that spike protein, and that's not a good thing for you... It's biologically active, initiates biological processes, and causes certain body functions to be totally disrupted or even destroyed,' Yeadon repeated.

Effects of vaccines can strike after days, weeks, months or even years

It depends on the immune system of the person and the reaction of his cells to the genetic instructions whether these effects occur immediately, in the short term, or only in the medium or long term. So, people who are vaccinated now and say 'nothing will happen' are definitely not safe. The effects can strike tomorrow, next month, next year, or even after a few years. If I were a (medical) institution I would no longer provide these vaccines,' Yeadon emphasized.

Meanwhile, tens of millions of Europeans and more than 100 million Americans have already been injected with them, and it doesn't look like politicians are even going to consider whether these "vaccines" packaged as genetic engineering are really as "safe" as the manufacturers claim.

Dr. Füllmich then reiterated Yeadon's words that the "vaccines" now being dispensed are in reality not vaccines, but "something completely different. It is only classified as a vaccine because it is used as a vaccine.' However, they are not vaccines, but substances that amount to gene therapy, to genetic manipulation. The worst thing is that a great many (serious) side effects may not be linked to these substances, precisely because they are falsely used as 'vaccines'.

'First step is awareness, second step: take action'

Can we still stop this? 'Awareness is the first step of resistance,' Koire says. 'Action is the second step.' People need to understand that we are now conditioned to remain passive, and to think that if we press 'like' on social media, we are politically active. 'But you're not a political activist if you don't leave your house.' Hence all these lockdowns and social distancing - they want to declare mass opposition to this Agenda 21 demolition and total control plan illegal and impossible in advance.

'And don't say that your government is so bad that there's nothing you can do about it. I'm sure it looks that way, but that's because you've let it get this far. It won't get any better if you just let this go on. That's why we think you really need to "occupy" your government (occupy, also "seize," "occupy," or "occupy"). BE your government. Yes, we are in the End Game, and there is not much time left. So, you should have done this a while ago.'

People need to start recognizing Agenda 21, even in their own locality and region. Bring it up in your local council. Continuously talk to representatives of the people about it. Probably every item on your city council's agenda is linked to Agenda 21.' She advises people to look at her website and read her book so that 'you're going to find out how they manipulate public opinion, so you're not going to cause problems for them. They want you to stay home in your chair.'

So, take action, speak to people and officials, hand out flyers, share videos, write and publish about it. 'Because just knowing that this is going on, without doing anything about it, is not enough anymore. You have to become politically active and be prepared not to immediately take over everything from them.' For example, they want to start replacing reality with VR (virtual reality), because it would make life so much more fun.'But as soon as you start doing that, your life is over. So, you have to resist.'

Don't believe Wikipedia, Agenda-21 is an anti-human agenda

'Wherever you work, wherever you are, talk about this.' Many people won't like that, and won't like you (anymore). But so be it, because this plan is real, and is being implemented right now, whether we like it or not. 'Agenda 21 is NOT what Wikipedia tells you. It is NOT voluntary, and not 'non-binding'. For you, this plan is mandatory.... So let's fight this together. We must all oppose it.'

They are selling it as something that will improve and save the world, the climate, the environment. But (Agenda 21 / 2030) is an anti-human agenda this is being implemented right now. We don't want to go down that dark path, this path to tyranny.'

Our other books

Check out our other books for other unreported news, exposed facts and debunked truths, and more.

Join the exclusive Rebel Press Media Circle!

You will get a new updates about the unreported reality delivered in your inbox every Friday.

Sign up here today:

https://campsite.bio/rebelpressmedia

www.ingramcontent.com/pod-product-compliance
Lightning Source LLC
Chambersburg PA
CBHW061313140726
47998CB00006B/2368